1 Introduction

A fundamental question in empirical asset pricing is the effect of firm characteristics on stock returns. The proportion of a firm's output that is exported abroad, referred to as "tradability" in this paper, is an important degree of firm heterogeneity that has not been studied in asset pricing.[1] As globalization increases, firms' capability to trade their output becomes an increasingly significant attribute. This paper examines how the tradability of a firm's output impacts its stock returns.

I document that firms in the tradable sector have more cyclical asset returns and earnings than firms in the non-tradable sector. I argue that the empirical patterns are driven by the adjustment of the relative price of tradable to non-tradable goods, primarily due to supply shocks that hit the economy. Business cycles impact the returns of firms in the tradable sector differently than the returns of firms in the non-tradable sector. A tradable good, by definition, can be traded across countries while the non-tradable good can only be consumed at home. The price of a tradable good is determined in the international market, based on the aggregate supply and demand of the good from domestic and foreign countries, while the price of the non-tradable good is determined solely based on domestic supply and demand. Therefore, from the perspective of the domestic country, the equilibrium price of the tradable good will react relatively less than the price of the non-tradable good to shocks that hit the domestic economy because the tradable good price also depends on foreign shocks. This is referred to as the *relative price adjustment mechanism*.

This implies that during bad times at home, when a negative supply shock hits both sectors of the U.S. economy (e.g. a natural disaster disrupts productivity), equilibrium prices will go up, but will go up less for the tradable good than the non-tradable good. As

---

[1] Goods with a relatively high and low degree of tradability are called "tradable" and "non-tradable" respectively.

a result, the relative price of the tradable good, defined to be the ratio of the tradable good price to the non-tradable good price, will fall, leading to lower relative cash flows for the tradable sector. Hence, stock returns in the tradable sector will be lower than stock returns in the non-tradable sector during bad times. Conversely, when a positive supply shock hits the economy in good times, stock returns in the tradable sector will be higher. In essence, the relative price adjustment makes the tradable sector *more* exposed to supply shocks.

A simple two-country endowment economy model formalizes the intuition and links the relative price of the tradable good with asset returns, cash flows, and the real exchange rate. Following the international real business cycle literature, fluctuations in the model are driven by exogenous shocks to endowment.[2] The model generates three testable implications which are confirmed in the empirical findings. From the perspective of the domestic country, (1) firms in the tradable sector have more cyclical returns; (2) firms in the tradable sector have more volatile earnings growth; and (3) returns of a long short portfolio of firms in the tradable versus non-tradable sector predict the real dollar exchange rate.

I test the model's predictions in the data by classifying industries based on the tradability of their output. Using the 2002 Bureau of Economic Analysis's National Income and Product Account (BEA NIPA) Input-Output Tables, I compute a tradability ratio, defined to be the value of exports over the total industry output, for over 400 industries in the United States. Firms are sorted into five portfolios based on their industry's tradability ratio. Firms in the top and bottom quintile of tradability are designated as the tradable and non-tradable sector respectively. I then construct a tradable minus non-tradable portfolio ($TMNT$) of stock returns, defined to be the difference in value-weighted returns of firms in the tradable and non-tradable sector.

In the empirical results, I find strong support for the relative price adjustment mechanism

---

[2]Baxter (1995) and Crucini (2008) contain an extensive survey of this area.

due to supply shocks. In particular, firms that produce tradable goods have more cyclical asset returns than firms that produce non-tradable goods, where cyclicality is measured as the beta from regressing excess returns on GDP growth. GDP betas monotonically increase across the tradability-sorted portfolios, indicating that higher tradability implies more exposure to GDP fluctuations. The results become even more striking when conditioned on periods of the business cycle. During NBER expansion periods, firms in the tradable sector on average outperform firms in the non-tradable sector by 3.8 percent per annum, while during NBER recession periods, they underperform them by almost 11 percent per annum. These effects persist even after controlling for the CAPM and Fama and French (1993) three-factor model, where the conditional alpha from these regressions is over negative 7 percent per annum for the $TMNT$ portfolio during recessions. These findings indicate that the tradability of a firm's output is a statistically and economically significant attribute that impacts the cyclicality of its stock returns.

Furthermore, the tradability of a firm's output also impacts the cyclicality of its earnings growth. Firms that produce tradable goods have more cyclical earnings growth than firms that produce non-tradable goods. This pattern is documented for three different measures of earnings: income, earnings per share, and return on assets (ROA). Firms in the top quintile of tradability are substantially more sensitive to business cycles than firms in the bottom quintile; their earnings fall the most during recessions and grow the most during expansions relative to the other quintiles. In particular, the earnings growth volatility of the tradable sector is 2.5 to 5 times that of the non-tradable sector, depending on the earnings measure. These patterns mirror the effects of tradability on average stock returns.

An important contribution in the paper is documenting the predictability of the real dollar exchange rate. The empirical predictive literature uses primarily macroeconomic variables to predict the real exchange rate.[3] In contrast, I use asset returns. The advantage of using

---

[3]See Rossi (2013) for a survey of the literature.

asset returns is that they are updated at a higher frequency, and their forward-looking nature can capture expected movements in the productivities of the tradable and non-tradable sectors. Hence, asset returns can pick up on fluctuations in the real exchange rate that otherwise may not be detected by slower-moving macroeconomic variables. In particular, I find that $TMNT$ significantly predicts real dollar exchange rate changes over horizons of 1 to 14 quarters ahead. The coefficient converges to 0.4 after eight quarters, indicating a one percent increase in the quarterly return of $TMNT$ implies a 0.4 percent appreciation of the U.S. dollar eight quarters ahead.

I consider the possibility that demand shocks rather than supply shocks may play a role in generating the empirical results. However, demand shocks generate implications in the opposite direction: when there is a negative demand shock during bad times (e.g. consumer wealth decreases leading to lower demand for goods), equilibrium prices in both the tradable and non-tradable sector will decrease, but will decrease less for the tradable good because of the relative price adjustment mechanism. As a result, the relative price of the tradable good will go up, and the tradable sector's stock returns will outperform the non-tradable sector's stock returns in bad times. In other words, while the relative price adjustment mechanism makes the tradable sector more exposed to supply shocks, it makes it *less* exposed to demand shocks because the tradable sector can hedge demand shocks at home by selling more or less abroad. While demand shocks presumably play a role in generating business cycles, the direction of the empirical results indicate the effects of business cycle supply shocks dominate the effects of business cycle demand shocks.

This paper is organized as follows. Section 2 discusses related literature. Section 3 provides a simple endowment economy model illustrating how tradability can impact asset prices. Section 4 documents the empirical patterns, which are consistent with the model. Section 5 verifies the results are robust to the tradability ratio changing over time and are not driven by the type of good produced. Section 6 concludes.

2 Related Literature

This paper links the areas of asset pricing and international economics, by examining the effects of the tradability of output on producing firms' stock returns. In addition, it contributes to the exchange rate predictability literature.

The paper is related to an extensive literature in asset pricing on connecting asset returns to fundamental aspects of firm heterogeneity. In general, papers in this area identify ex-ante sectors that may have different risk exposures due to characteristics of its economic activity or firm fundamentals. The particular firm characteristics examined vary widely across the literature. Subrahmanyam (2010), Harvey, Liu, and Zhu (2014), and Lewellen (2014) contain an extensive survey of firm characteristics that have been linked with stock returns. However, as far as I know, the tradability of a firm's output is an important degree of firm heterogeneity that has not been examined in the empirical asset pricing literature. This paper is related to Gomes, Kogan, and Yogo (2009), who examine the effect of the durability of output on expected stock returns. They find that firms that produce durable goods have greater exposure to systematic risk than firms that produce nondurable goods and services. While the durability of output and the tradability of output have a natural correlation, I find in Section 5.2 that durability is not the driving factor behind the tradability results.

A vast literature in international open macroeconomics and the real business cycle literature has looked at the differences of tradable and non-tradable goods. The classical papers in this area recognized that tradable and non-tradable sectors adjust differently to shocks that impact the economy. Starting with Cairnes (1874), these include Salter (1959), Swan (1960), Dornbusch (1980). Numerous papers have studied the differential effects of tradable versus non-tradable goods on firms' labor choice, capital investment, production, and resource allocations. However, few papers in this area have looked at the empirical impact of tradability on firms' asset returns.

This paper also contributes to the exchange rate predictability literature. Rossi (2013) contains a recent survey of the empirical literature that traditionally uses economic models and macroeconomic predictors. The random walk model consistently provides the toughest benchmark for these predictive models to beat. I take a different approach and use the difference in stock returns between firms with high and low tradability ratios to forecast exchange rates.

3   Endowment Economy Model

In this section, I present a two-country endowment economy model that demonstrates how tradability can affect firms' asset returns via the relative price adjustment mechanism. The model generates three testable implications: (1) firms in the tradable sector have more cyclical returns; (2) firms in the tradable sector have more volatile cash flow growth; and (3) returns of a long short portfolio of firms in the tradable versus non-tradable sector significantly predict the real exchange rate.

3.1   Setup

The model builds on a Lucas (1982) endowment economy with two countries Home and Foreign. Each country has two sectors: a tradable and a non-tradable sector. There are three types of goods: one tradable good that is freely and costlessly traded across countries and one non-tradable good in each country. The non-tradable good can only be consumed in the domestic market.

Embedded in the setup is the relative price adjustment mechanism, the notion that from the perspective of the domestic country, the equilibrium price of the tradable good will react relatively less than the price of the non-tradable good to shocks that hit the domestic economy, because the tradable good price also depends on foreign shocks. Without loss of generality, the tradable good is set to be the numeraire with a price of 1, while the relative price of the non-tradable good in the Home and Foreign country is p_H and p_F respectively. Asset markets are assumed to be complete.

In each country, there exists a continuum of identical households with constant relative risk aversion γ. Utility at time t in country $i \in H, F$ is

$$U(c_t^i) = \frac{1}{1-\gamma}(c_t^i)^{1-\gamma} \tag{1}$$

where c_t^i is a constant elasticity of substitution (CES) consumption bundle:

$$c_t^i = [\theta(c_{T,t}^i)^\tau + (1-\theta)(c_{NT,t}^i)^\tau]^{\frac{1}{\tau}}. \tag{2}$$

$c_{T,t}^i$ and $c_{NT,t}^i$ is the consumption of the tradable and non-tradable good. θ is the weight of the tradable good in the consumption basket, while $\epsilon \equiv \frac{1}{1-\tau}$ is the elasticity of substitution between the tradable and non-tradable good.

The price of the consumption bundle in terms of the numeraire, the tradable good, is

$$P_t^i = [\theta^\epsilon + (1-\theta)^\epsilon(p_{i,t})^{1-\epsilon}]^{\frac{1}{1-\epsilon}} \tag{3}$$

where the price index is defined as the minimum expenditure such that $c_t^i = 1$.

$x_{j,t}^i$ is the endowment of good $j \in T, NT$ at time t in country i, which follows a mean-reverting stochastic process

$$\mathrm{d}x_{j,t}^i = -\theta_{x,j}^i(x_{j,t}^i - \bar{x}_j^i)\mathrm{d}t + \sigma_{x,j}^i\mathrm{d}Z_{j,t}^i \tag{4}$$

where

$$\mathrm{d}Z_{j,t}^{H} \cdot \mathrm{d}Z_{k,t}^{F} = 0$$

$$\mathrm{d}Z_{j,t}^{i} \cdot \mathrm{d}Z_{k,t}^{i} = \delta_{x}^{i} \mathrm{d}t$$

Endowment shocks within a country have correlation δ_{x}^{i}, while shocks across countries are independent. $\theta_{x,j}^{i}$ is the rate at which the shock reverts toward mean $\bar{x}_{j}^{i}$; $\sigma_{x,j}^{i}$ is the volatility of the shock.

3.2   Equilibrium

Under the assumption of complete markets, the competitive equilibrium can be obtained by solving the world social planner's problem, contained in Appendix B. As seen in equations (28) and (29), equilibrium prices $p_{H,t}$ and $p_{F,t}$ cannot be written in terms of state variables in closed-form and must be solved for numerically by performing a model calibration.

Table 1 contains the parameters used for the calibration. I use a discount rate of $\rho = 0.005$ for quarterly data and a coefficient of relative risk aversion γ of 5. The elasticity of substitution ϵ is set to 1 so that the tradable and non-tradable good are imperfect substitutes, consistent with previous papers.[4] The consumption bundle comprises an equal weight on each good. The weight on the Home country in the social planner problem, λ, is set to 0.5, roughly the share of U.S. to total G7 GDP.

Parameters for the endowment processes for the Home and Foreign country are calibrated to match actual data from 1950-2007 for the U.S. and the rest of the G7 countries respectively. Quarterly data for the U.S. is from the BEA NIPA tables and for the G7 countries (excluding U.S.) is from the International Monetary Fund's International Financial Statistics (IMF IFS)

---

[4]See Stockman and Tesar (1995), Lewis (1996), and Ostry and Reinhart (1992).

database. The mean reversion rate and volatility of endowment shocks in the tradable and non-tradable sector match that in the detrended quantities of exports and quantities of GDP series respectively.[5] Correlation of shocks to the tradable and non-tradable sector within a country match the correlation of the detrended exports and GDP series.

3.3 Model Predictions

The model's predictions are from the perspective of the Home country.

Model Prediction 1: Stock returns of the tradable sector are more cyclical.

Model Prediction 2: Cash flow growth in the tradable sector is more volatile.

Table 2 presents the model simulation results of stock returns and cash flow growth for the Home country. Using the calibration parameters, I generate endowment processes with a length of 50 years. The simulated data is at a quarterly frequency and then aggregated to form annual observations. For each variable, the table shows the median, 5th, and 95th percentile values over 1000 Monte Carlo simulations.

The results in panel A show that returns in the tradable sector are more volatile than returns in the non-tradable sector; the median standard deviation over simulations is 22.3 percent versus 15.6 percent annually. To compare the cyclicality of the returns, I examine the ratio of the covariance of returns and output growth in the two sectors:

$$\frac{\operatorname{cov}(\frac{\mathrm{d}S_{T,t}^H}{S_{T,t}^H}, \mathrm{d}X_t^H)}{\operatorname{cov}(\frac{\mathrm{d}S_{NT,t}^H}{S_{NT,t}^H}, \mathrm{d}X_t^H)} \tag{5}$$

where $X_t^H = x_{T,t}^H + p_{H,T}x_{NT,t}^H$ is the total output in the Home country. The results show

---

[5]Data series are detrended using the Hodrick-Prescott filter (Hodrick and Prescott 1997) to more closely represent a mean-reverting endowment process as in equation (4).

that the covariance in the tradable sector is 1.7 times as high as that in the non-tradable sector. Panel B shows that cash flow growth in the tradable sector is more volatile; its volatility is roughly 1.2 times as high as the volatility in the non-tradable sector for the median simulation.

The intuition for the results arise from the relative price adjustment mechanism: the equilibrium price of the tradable good will react relatively less than the price of the non-tradable good to Home endowment shocks, because the tradable good price also depends on Foreign endowment shocks. This implies that during bad times in the Home country, when a negative endowment shock hits both sectors, equilibrium prices will go up, but will go up less for the tradable good than the non-tradable good. As a result, the relative price of the non-tradable good, $p_{H,T}$ (since the price of the tradable good is normalized to 1), will increase. In the model, cash flow in each sector is equal to its endowment times price:

$$d_{T,t}^{H} = x_{T,t}^{H} \cdot 1, \quad d_{NT,t}^{H} = x_{NT,t}^{H} \cdot p_{H,t}. \tag{6}$$

If we compare the cash flows of the two sectors, controlling for endowment shock size, the non-tradable sector will suffer less because its equilibrium price will increase. Put another way, during bad times, the tradable sector will suffer more than the non-tradable sector since its cash flow will fall more. Since stock prices for each sector are equal to the present discounted value of its future cash flow, asset returns will also be lower in the tradable sector. In essence, the relative price adjustment makes the tradable sector more exposed to endowment shocks, leading to more volatile cash flow growth and more cyclical stock returns.

Model Prediction 3: The difference in returns between the tradable and non-tradable sector can predict the exchange rate.

In an endowment economy, the real exchange rate between the Home and Foreign country is defined as the ratio of their price indices P_t^i (defined in equation (3)),

$$RER_t = \frac{P_t^H}{P_t^F} \tag{7}$$

where an increase in RER signifies an appreciation of the Home currency.

The model allows us to examine the link between stock returns and the exchange rate. RER_t moves as equilibrium prices $p_{H,t}$ and $p_{F,t}$ move. The difference in returns between the tradable and non-tradable sector is related to differences in future expected cash flows, which depend on endowments and also equilibrium prices $p_{H,t}$ and $p_{F,t}$. Therefore, the difference in returns between the two sectors should be able to predict future movements in the real exchange rate.

Using model-simulated data, I regress the forward-looking change in real exchange rates on the Home country's returns of the $TMNT$ portfolio, the difference in returns between the tradable (T) and non-tradable (NT) sector, for horizons of $h = 1$ to 16 quarters:

$$\log(RER)_{t+h} - \log(RER)_t = \alpha_h + \beta_h R_{TMNT,t}^H + \epsilon_t \tag{8}$$

$$\log(RER)_{t+h} - \log(RER)_t = \alpha_h + \gamma_{T,h} R_{T,t}^H + \gamma_{NT,h} R_{NT,t}^H + \epsilon_t \tag{9}$$

Equation (9) splits the right hand side into the returns of the tradable and non-tradable sector separately.

Figure 1 presents the results. The solid line is the median coefficient, and the dotted lines are the 5th and 95th percentile coefficients over all simulations. Panel A plots the coefficient on the returns of the $TMNT$ portfolio. $TMNT$ is a significant predictor at the one percent level of the real exchange rate change over horizons of 2 to 16 quarters. The coefficient converges roughly to 0.4 after nine quarters, indicating that a one percent increase in the quarterly return of $TMNT$ will result in a 0.4 percent appreciation of the Home currency relative to the Foreign currency. Panels B and C plot the coefficients on the T and NT portfolio. The signs indicate a significant positive loading on the returns of the tradable portfolio and a significant negative loading on the returns of the non-tradable portfolio.

4   Empirical Results

In this section, I empirically test the predictions of the model. The model's predictions hold in the data, providing strong support for the relative price adjustment mechanism due to supply shocks. The empirical patterns go against the intuition for demand shocks.

4.1   Measuring the Tradability Ratio of Output

In order to examine the empirical implications of the tradability of output on firms' stock returns, I classify industries based on the tradability of their output. I use the 2002 Bureau of Economic Analysis's National Income and Product Account (BEA NIPA) Input-Output Tables to compute a tradability ratio for over 400 industries in the US. This ratio is defined to be the value of exports for the industry over the total industry output. I use the Make and Usage Tables within the Input-Output Tables to compute this measure. The Make Table shows the value of the output produced by each of the 439 industries of each of the 431 listed commodities. The Usage Table shows how each produced commodity is used: how much of it is used by each industry and how much is used toward final uses such as exports, imports, consumption, investment, and government spending. Combining these two tables, I compute the proportion of the total industry output that is exported abroad, which I call the tradability ratio.[6]

The top and bottom ten industries by tradability ratio from the dataset are listed in

---

[6]This methodology follows Goldstein and Officer (1979), Goldstein, Khan, and Officer (1980), Kravis and Lipsey (1988), Gregorio, Giovannini, and Wolf (1994), and Bems (2008).

Table 3. The top ten industries consist almost entirely of various manufacturing industries. "Optical instrument and lens manufacturing" is the industry with the highest tradability ratio, exporting 88 percent of its output. The fishing industry is the only top ten industry that is not in manufacturing and exports 74 percent of its output. On the other hand, industries in the botton ten export essentially none of their products. Many are services industries, including car washes and various personal care services. In Section 5.2, I verify that the durability of goods is not driving my tradability results.

Since the tradability ratio is available at the industry level, I map each firm in the Center for Research in Securities Prices (CRSP) Monthly Stock Database to its respective industry, thus obtaining a tradability ratio for each firm. After dropping all firms in the financial sector (SIC 6000-6999) and firms missing a NAICS industry code, 14,190 firms remain. Appendix A contains the full details of the dataset and tradability classification at the industry and firm level.

Table 4 contains the summary statistics for the tradability ratio over all 439 industries and 14,190 firms. The statistics for both columns are essentially identical, a good indication that results are not driven by a few industries with a large number of firms. Half of U.S. industries export more than 5.5 percent of their total output; 20 percent export more than 17 percent of their total output.

4.2 Cyclicality of Tradability-Sorted Portfolios

I test the first prediction in the model, that stock returns in the tradable sector are more cyclical. To examine the effect of tradability on stock returns, I sort the 14,190 firms into five portfolios based on their tradability ratio. I label firms in quintile one as the non-tradable (NT) sector and firms in quintile five as the tradable (T) sector.

Table 5 presents the average firm-level characteristics for each portfolio over the period

1950-2007. There are 2,838 firms in each portfolio. The number of industries that comprise each portfolio ranges from 52 to 93. Data on firm-level characteristics are from Compustat. The spread in tradability ratio is much larger in the T portfolio (quintile 5) than in the other portfolios: quintile one through four have tradability ratio that ranges from zero to 18 percent, while quintile five has tradability ratio that ranges from 18 to 88 percent. The share of total market equity varies from 9 to 20 percent. Together the five portfolios contain about 67 percent of the total market equity of all firms in CRSP, indicating the tradability classification of firms includes the vast majority of firms in the CRSP universe. Both book-to-market and leverage exhibit a weakly decreasing pattern, as firms with higher tradability tend to have lower book-to-market and leverage. However, this spread across portfolios is small.

I construct a tradable minus non-tradable portfolio (denoted as $TMNT$) of monthly stock returns, defined to be the difference in value-weighted excess returns of firms in quintile five (T) and quintile one (NT). As a robustness check, I also construct $TMNT_2$, equal to the value-weighted excess returns of firms in quintile five minus the value-weighted excess returns of firms in quintiles one through four. Data on monthly returns and shares outstanding are from CRSP. Data on the risk-free rate is from Ken French's website.

Table 6 shows the average monthly excess returns, t-statistics, and standard deviation for the five tradability-sorted portfolios, $TMNT$, and $TMNT_2$. Over the entire sample period of 1950-2007, $TMNT$ has an average return of 0.14 percent per month or roughly 1.7 percent per year, consistent with the model simulation results in Table 2, where $TMNT$ has a return of roughly 2 percent per year. Also consistent with the model is the fact that the return volatility of the T portfolio (6 percent a month) is higher than the return volatility of the NT portfolio (3.8 percent a month). In fact, return volatility for the sorted portfolios increases with tradability.

This pattern is more apparent when the sample period is split into recession and expansion

14

periods, where recession dates are based on business cycles as determined by the NBER. In particular, $TMNT$ has an average return of negative 0.9 percent a month or almost negative 11 percent a year during recessions, compared with an average return of 0.3 percent a month or 3.8 percent a year during expansions. The t-statistics for these returns are significant. Consistent with the model's prediction, this shows that the returns of tradable firms are significantly more sensitive to business cycles than non-tradable firms. Tradable firms earn higher returns than non-tradable firms during periods of expansions and earn substantially lower returns during recessions. Averages for $TMNT_2$ are comparable to $TMNT$; the two portfolios have correlation of 0.91 over the sample period. Figure 2 plots the annual returns of $TMNT$ going back to 1927 with the NBER-dated recessions shaded in. The picture is striking: not only does the pattern hold for average returns, but $TMNT$ has consistently negative returns during nearly each recession and positive returns during each expansion.

Due to the link between the returns of the tradability-sorted portfolios and business cycles, I run conditional CAPM and Fama and French (1993) three-factor time series regressions in Table 7 to check that the return patterns are not explained by these benchmark factor models. Panel A presents the results from the monthly conditional CAPM regression over the sample period 1950-2007:

$$R_{i,t} = \alpha_i + \alpha_{i,rec}d_{rec,t} + \beta_i^{MKT}R_{MKT,t} + \beta_{i,rec}^{MKT}(R_{MKT,t} \cdot d_{rec,t}) + \epsilon_t \tag{10}$$

where $d_{rec,t}$ is a dummy variable that is equal to 1 if the economy is in a recession during month t and equal to 0 otherwise. The results indicate that unconditional CAPM alphas (α_i) are insignificant across all portfolios. However, during recessions, conditional CAPM alphas ($\alpha_{i,rec}$) monotonically decrease with tradability, ranging from 0.4 percent a month for the NT portfolio to negative 0.2 percent a month for the T portfolio. $TMNT$ has a statistically significant conditional CAPM alpha of negative 0.6 percent a month or equivalently negative 7.5 percent a year in returns that cannot be explained by CAPM. Market betas increase

15

monotonically across portfolios, with $TMNT$ having a market beta of 0.41, but this cannot explain the spread in returns during recessions. The small and insignificant magnitudes of $\beta_{i,rec}^{MKT}$ indicate that the portfolios' exposure to the market is not conditional on the business cycle.

Panel B presents the results from the conditional Fama French three-factor regression:

$$R_{i,t} = \alpha_i + \alpha_{i,rec} d_{rec,t} + \beta_i^{MKT} R_{MKT,t} + \beta_{i,rec}^{MKT}(R_{MKT,t} \cdot d_{rec,t}) + \quad (11)$$

$$\beta_i^{SMB} R_{SMB,t} + \beta_{i,rec}^{SMB}(R_{SMB,t} \cdot d_{rec,t}) + \beta_i^{HML} R_{HML,t} + \beta_{i,rec}^{HML}(R_{HML,t} \cdot d_{rec,t}) + \epsilon_t$$

The results are similar to the CAPM regression as the unconditional alpha is insignificant across portfolios, while the conditional alpha during recessions is monotonically decreasing with tradability. Even after accounting for the three Fama French factors, $TMNT$ still has a negative 0.6 percent a month or over negative 7 percent a year in returns during recessions that cannot be explained. $TMNT$ has a market beta of 0.26, SMB beta of 0.3, and HML beta of -0.32. The tradability-sorted portfolios' exposure to these three factors does not depend on the business cycle, as conditional betas are insignificant. This shows that return patterns in $TMNT$ cannot be explained by market, size, or book-to-market factors.

A potential concern with the conditional regressions is that conditioning on the NBER recession dates may be using forward-looking information that is not available at the time of the stock return. I repeat the regressions by conditioning instead on the past two quarters' GDP growth, where a recession is two consecutive quarters of negative growth, and the results are the same (not shown).

The previous results indicate the sensitivity of the T portfolio relative to the NT portfolio to business cycles. The most direct comparison is to compare the cyclicality of the tradability-sorted portfolios. Table 8 measures the exposure of portfolios to business cycles, by computing their GDP beta. GDP beta is the coefficient from regressing the excess returns on the contemporaneous change in real GDP per capita. Data on GDP and consumption is from BEA NIPA Table 1.1.6. Returns are converted to a quarterly frequency to match the frequency of GDP.

The GDP beta is statistically significant and increases monotonically with tradability, with a small spread among the four lower quintiles and a large increase for the tradable portfolio. The GDP beta of 2.11 for the T portfolio is more than twice the GDP beta for the NT portfolio, indicating that on average the returns of tradable firms are more than twice as cyclical as the returns of non-tradable firms. The GDP beta for $TMNT$ is 1.2 and significant.

The empirical results clearly support the model's first prediction that returns in the tradable sector are more cyclical than returns in the non-tradable sector, providing evidence for the relative price adjustment mechanism due to supply shocks presented in the model. In essence, the relative price adjustment of tradable versus non-tradable good prices make the tradable sector more exposed to supply shocks. On the other hand, the empirical patterns go in the opposite direction as implied by the relative price adjustment mechanism due to demand shocks, since the tradable sector is less exposed to business cycles due to demand shocks because the tradable sector can hedge demand shocks at home by selling more or less abroad.

4.3   Earnings Growth of Tradability-Sorted Portfolios

I test the model's second prediction about the effect of tradability on earnings growth. I examine the earnings of the tradability-sorted portfolios, and find that earnings growth in the tradable sector is more cyclical and volatile than that in the non-tradable sector, echoing the results with stock returns and consistent with the model's prediction.

Table 9 presents the average annual change in earnings growth for the tradability-sorted portfolios. I use three different measures of earnings: income before extraordinary items, earnings per share, and return on assets (ROA), which is income over total assets. Data for these variables is from Compustat, available at a quarterly frequency from 1961-2007.

Panel A reports the mean and standard deviation of the annual growth rate of income. Over the sample period 1961-2007, the growth rate is increasing with tradability, where NT firms have an average income growth rate of 18 percent versus 26 percent for T firms. The standard deviation increases with tradability as well, 16 percent for NT firms compared with 40 percent for T firms. Over recession periods, the growth rate of income decreases with tradability. The pattern is reversed over expansion periods, where income for the T sector increases 30 percent annually, compared with 18 percent for the NT sector. These patterns show that income growth in the tradable sector is substantially more volatile and more sensitive to business cycles than the non-tradable sector: its income falls the most during recessions and grows the most during expansions.

Average statistics for the annual growth rate of earnings per share are shown in Panel B. The patterns are similar, in that during expansions, the growth rate of earnings per share is highest for T firms, lowest for NT firms, and increases with tradability. The direction is again reversed when looking at only recession periods, where earnings per share for T firms drop 15 percent versus an increase of 5 percent for NT firms. In fact, the volatility of earnings growth for the tradable sector (63 percent per annum) is significantly higher than that for the non-tradable sector (12 percent per annum), roughly five times as high over the sample period.

Panel C presents the results for the average annual change in ROA. These numbers exhibit consistent patterns with income and earnings per share. The difference in average growth rates of ROA between recession and expansion periods provides evidence of the impact of business cycles on each sector's earnings. This difference increases with tradability and provides strong evidence that the earnings of tradable firms are substantially more volatile and cyclical than the earnings of non-tradable firms.

4.4 Predictability of the Real Exchange Rate

I document that the third prediction in the model, that the relative price adjustment mechanism implies the difference in stock returns between the tradable and non-tradable sector is predictive of the real dollar exchange rate, holds in the data. An important contribution of the paper is finding evidence of exchange rate predictability using stock returns. Traditional real exchange rate models use macroeconomic variables such as GDP, monetary policy, purchasing power parity (PPP), or labor markets to predict fluctuations in real exchange rate. The advantage of using asset returns is that they are updated at a higher frequency, and their forward-looking nature can capture expected movements in the productivities of the tradable and non-tradable sectors. Hence, asset returns can pick up on fluctuations in the real exchange rate that otherwise may not be detected by slower-moving macroeconomic variables.

Following previous work, I define the real dollar exchange rate, in terms of the number of foreign currency units per U.S. dollar, as follows:[7]

$$RER_t = \prod_i RER_{i,t}^{GDPwt_{i,t}} \tag{12}$$

where

$$RER_{i,t} = NER_{i,t} * \frac{P_{H,t}}{P_{i,t}}$$

$$GDPwt_{i,t} = \frac{GDP_{i,t}}{\sum_i GDP_{i,t}}$$

$NER_{i,t}$ is the nominal bilateral exchange rate between the U.S. and foreign country i, $\frac{P_{H,t}}{P_{i,t}}$

---

[7]Dornbusch (1980), Frenkel and Mussa (1985), Edwards (1989), Zietz (1996)

is the ratio of the CPI between the U.S. and foreign country i, and $GDPwt_{i,t}$ is the ratio of country i's GDP to the total GDP for all foreign countries. The real exchange rate is then the GDP-weighted average of the real bilateral exchange rate between the U.S. and all foreign countries i. In my construction, I let i be the six foreign countries that are part of the G7: Canada, France, Germany, Italy, Japan, and the United Kingdom. Data on nominal exchange rates, CPI, and GDP are from the International Monetary Fund's International Financial Statistics (IMF IFS) database. The resulting series for the real exchange rate is available at a quarterly frequency from 1968-2007.[8]

I regress the forward-looking change in real exchange rate on the returns of the $TMNT$ portfolio:

$$\log(RER)_{t+h} - \log(RER)_t = \alpha_h + \beta_h R_{TMNT,t} + \epsilon_t \tag{13}$$

$$\log(RER)_{t+h} - \log(RER)_t = \alpha_h + \gamma_{T,h} R_{T,t} + \gamma_{NT,h} R_{NT,t} + \epsilon_t \tag{14}$$

where $R_{TMNT,t}$ are quarterly returns of $TMNT$. Equation (14) splits the right hand side variable into R_T and R_{NT}, returns on the tradable and non-tradable portfolio respectively. I estimate the regression for real exchange rate change over horizons of $h = 1$ to 16 quarters. Since the real exchange rate is in terms of the number of foreign currency units per U.S. dollar, an increase in the exchange rate means an appreciation of the U.S. dollar.

Figure 3 plots the coefficients for R_{TMNT}, R_T, and R_{NT} respectively (solid lines), along with the one and two standard error confidence intervals (dashed lines). The t-statistics are estimated using Newey and West (1987) standard errors, to adjust for autocorrelation and heteroskedasticity. $TMNT$ is a significant predictor at the five percent level of real exchange rate change over horizons of 1 to 14 quarters. The coefficient on R_{TMNT} converges to 0.4

---

[8]The IMF IFS contains data on its own real effective exchange rate (REER) with respect to the U.S., which is a weighted average of a basket of foreign currencies. Results with this series are similar.

after eight quarters, similar in magnitude to the model simulation results in Figure 1. This indicates that a one percent increase in the quarterly return of $TMNT$ will result in a 0.4 percent appreciation of the U.S. dollar relative to foreign currencies of the G7 eight quarters ahead. When the $TMNT$ portfolio is separated into the returns of the T and NT portfolio, we see that most of the significance is coming from the tradable portfolio, rather than the non-tradable portfolio.

In sum, the model's three testable implications are strongly supported in the empirical results, indicating that tradability is linked to asset returns, earnings, and the real exchange rate via the relative price of goods in the tradable and non-tradable sector. The direction of the results are consistent with the relative price adjustment mechanism due to supply shocks: negative supply shocks during recessions cause the price of the tradable good to fall relative to the price of the non-tradable good, leading to lower relative cash flows and stock returns; positive supply shocks during expansions lead to higher relative cash flows and stock returns for the tradable sector.

It is important to consider the possibility that demand shocks rather than supply shocks may play a role in generating the empirical results. However, demand shocks generate implications in the opposite direction: when there is a negative demand shock during recessions, the relative price of the tradable good will increase and the tradable sector will outperform the non-tradable sector. In other words, while the relative price adjustment mechanism makes the tradable sector more exposed to supply shocks, it makes it *less* exposed to demand shocks because the tradable sector can hedge demand shocks at home by selling more or less abroad. While demand shocks presumably play a role in generating business cycles, the direction of the empirical results indicate the effects of business cycle supply shocks dominate the effects of business cycle demand shocks.

5 Robustness of Results

5.1 Tradability Over Time

The tradability ratio, defined to be the amount of exports over the total output of the industry, is constructed using the 2002 BEA NIPA Input-Output Tables. One potential concern about the empirical results is that the sample period starts from 1950 and industries' tradability most likely will change over time. It would be ideal to construct a tradability ratio every year. However the Input-Output Tables are only available every five years starting from 1987.[9] As a robustness check, I rerun some of empirical results using the 1987 rather than the 2002 data as an alternative measure of tradability ratio.

Robustness Table 1 repeats the analysis in Table 4 using the 1987 BEA Table. There are 505 industries mapping to 18530 firms in CRSP. Half of U.S. industries export more than 3.3 percent of their total output, with 20 percent exporting more than 10.7 percent. Overall, the summary statistics show that the tradability of industries in 1987 is slightly lower than that in 2002. Average monthly excess returns for tradability-sorted portfolios, constructed using 1987 data, are shown in Robustness Table 2. In general the return patterns hold. $TMNT$ has an average return of negative 0.6 percent a month over recessions (negative 7.3 percent a year), compared with an average return of 0.3 percent a month over expansions (3.1 percent a year).

The return correlation matrix for the five tradability-sorted portfolios, created using 1987 versus 2002 data, is shown in Robustness Table 3. Overall, correlations between corresponding tradability-sorted portfolios (diagonal elements) are very high, all larger than 0.9. The correlation of the tradable minus non-tradable $TMNT$ portfolios is 0.94. Robustness Table

---

[9]The first available Input-Output Table with the Make and Use Tables is 1972. However, there is not an available mapping of the industries to their respective SIC codes for 1972. Since the CRSP/Compustat database assigns the 1987 SIC codes to firms, the 1987 Input-Output data is the earliest feasible table.

4 presents the portfolio transition probabilities. Row i column j shows the probability that a firm which was sorted into quintile i using 1987 tradability ends up in quintile j using 2002 tradability. 69 percent of the firms in the tradable sector (quintile 5) in 1987 are still in the tradable sector in 2002. 71 percent of the firms in the non-tradable sector (quintile 1) in 1987 are in the non-tradable sector in 2002. These transition probabilities indicate that tradability of output is a characteristic that is fairly stable over time.

5.2 Tradability Within Type of Good Produced

I examine the composition of the five portfolios sorted by tradability, by classifying the industries in each portfolio into one of the categories of final demand: durable good, nondurable good, services, gross private domestic investment, government consumption expenditures and gross investment, and net exports.[10] Consumption goods is comprised of the union of durable goods, nondurable goods, and services. I focus on the consumption and investment categories as they are the largest components of GDP.

I label each industry into either a consumption industry (durables, nondurables, services), investment industry, or other. I follow the mapping of SIC codes to a category of final demand contained in the appendix of Gomes, Kogan, and Yogo (2009). Robustness Table 5 contains the summary statistics. It provides the number of firms in each tradability-sorted portfolio that produce goods which fall into either a consumption or investment industry. I compute the proportion of total market capitalization of all firms in each category over the market capitalization of the portfolio.

A potential concern with the empirical results is that tradability ratio may be correlated with other firm characteristics that are driving the results. One natural candidate is the link between tradability and durability of output, since goods that are durable tend to

---

[10]See http://www.bea.gov for a precise definition of these categories.

be more tradable, while services tend to be non-tradable. It is not surprising to see in Robustness Table 5 that the number of durable firms that are in each portfolio increases with tradability, while the number of services firms decreases with tradability. However, durable firms only account for 2.5 percent of the market capitalization in the T portfolio. Services firms account for only 10.2 percent of the market capitalization in the NT portfolio. Given that the durability categories make up such a low proportion of the portfolios' market capitalization, it is unlikely that durability, instead of tradability, is driving the empirical results. Furthermore, the correlation of stock returns of $TMNT$ and a portfolio long on firms producing durable goods and short on firms producing services is essentially zero: it is -0.024 in the 1950-2007 sample period.

In addition, it is interesting to note that 45 percent of the firms in the T portfolio consist of investment-goods producing firms. A valid concern would be whether the T portfolio is just picking up attributes associated with investment-goods' producing firms and not actually effects due to tradability. I test this hypothesis in Robustness Table 6 by computing the GDP betas of firms in each tradability portfolio that are either in the consumption-goods or investment-goods industries. Within firms that produce consumption goods (labeled as C in the table), the T firms have GDP betas that are three times as high as that of the NT firms. Within firms that produce investment goods (labeled as I in the table), the most tradable firms actually have GDP betas that are significantly lower than the non-tradable firms, which is the opposite of the results in Table 8. Hence, it is unlikely that the investment firms in the T portfolio are driving the higher cyclicality of tradable firms. Of the firms in each portfolio that do not produce consumption goods (labeled as "not C") and do not produce investment goods (labeled as "not I"), we see similar GDP betas as the results with the entire portfolio. These patterns clearly indicate that the tradable portfolio's higher exposure to business cycle fluctuations relative to the non-tradable portfolio is not driven by the type of good produced.

6 Conclusion

In this paper, I examine the effect of the tradability of output on firms' stock returns. The dichotomy of goods into tradable versus non-tradable has long been part of the open economy macroeconomics literature, yet few papers have looked at the empirical implications of the tradability of output on asset returns. As international trade increases in the world economy, firms' capability to trade their output becomes an increasingly significant attribute.

I document that firms in the tradable sector have more cyclical asset returns and earnings than firms in the non-tradable sector. I argue that the empirical patterns are driven by the adjustment of the relative price of tradable to non-tradable goods, primarily due to supply shocks that hit the economy. A simple two-country endowment economy model formalizes the intuition behind the relative price adjustment mechanism and links the relative price of the tradable good with asset returns, cash flows, and the real exchange rate.

The model generates three testable implications which are confirmed in the empirical findings. From the perspective of the domestic country, (1) firms in the tradable sector have more cyclical returns; (2) firms in the tradable sector have more volatile earnings growth; and (3) returns of a long short portfolio of firms in the tradable versus non-tradable sector predict the dollar real exchange rate. The empirical results provide strong support for the relative price adjustment mechanism due to supply shocks.

References

BAXTER, M. (1995): "International trade and the business cycles," in *Handbook of International Economics*, vol. 3, pp. 1801–1864. Elsevier Science.

BEMS, R. (2008): "Aggregate investment expenditures on tradable and nontradable goods," *Review of Economic Dynamics*, 11, 852–883.

CAIRNES, J. (1874): *Some leading principles of political economy*. Harper and Brothers.

CRUCINI, M. (2008): "International real business cycles," in *The New Palgrave Dictionary of Economics*, vol. 2. Palgrave Macmillan.

DORNBUSCH, R. (1980): *Open economy macroeconomics*. Basic Books.

EDWARDS, S. (1989): *Real exchange rates, Devaluation, and Adjustment*. MIT Press.

FAMA, E. F., AND K. FRENCH (1993): "Common risk factors in the returns on stocks and bonds," *Journal of Financial Economics*, 33 (1), 3–56.

FRENKEL, J., AND M. MUSSA (1985): "Asset markets, exchange rates and the balance of payments," in *Handbook of International Economics*, vol. 2, pp. 679–747. Else.

GOLDSTEIN, M., M. KHAN, AND L. OFFICER (1980): "Prices of tradable and nontradable goods in the demand for total imports," *Review of Economics and Statistics*, 62 (2), 190–199.

GOLDSTEIN, M., AND L. OFFICER (1979): "New measures of prices and productivity for tradable and nontradable goods," *Review of Income and Wealth*, 25 (4), 413–427.

GOMES, J., L. KOGAN, AND M. YOGO (2009): "Durability of output and the cross-section of stock returns," *Journal of Political Economy*, 117, 941–986.

GREGORIO, J. D., A. GIOVANNINI, AND H. WOLF (1994): "International evidence on tradables and nontradables inflation," *European Economic Review*, 38, 1225–1244.

HARVEY, C. R., Y. LIU, AND H. ZHU (2014): "and the cross section of expected returns," NBER Working Paper Series.

HODRICK, R., AND E. PRESCOTT (1997): "Post-war U.S. Business cycles," *Journal of Money, Credit and Banking*, 29, 1–16.

KRAVIS, L., AND R. LIPSEY (1988): "National price levels and the prices of tradables and nontradables," *American Economic Review*, 78 (2), 474–478.

LEWELLEN, J. (2014): "The cross-section of expected stock returns," *Critical Finance Review*, forthcoming.

LEWIS, K. K. (1996): "What can explain the apparent lack of international consumption risk sharing?," *Journal of Political Economy*, 104 (2), 267–297.

LUCAS, R. (1982): "Interest rates and currency prices in a two-country world," *Journal of Monetary Economics*, 10, 335–359.

NEWEY, W. K., AND K. D. WEST (1987): "A simple, positive semi-definite heteroskedasticity and autocorrelation consistent covariance matrix," *Econometrica*, 55 (3), 703–708.

OSTRY, J. D., AND C. M. REINHART (1992): "Private saving and terms of trade shocks: evidence from developing countries," *International Monetary Fund Staff Papers*, 39 (3), 495–517.

ROSSI, B. (2013): "Exchange Rate Predictability," *Journal of Economic Literature*, 51 (4), 1063–1119.

SALTER, W. (1959): "International and external balance: the role of price and expenditure effects," *Economic Record*, 35, 226–238.

STEWART, R., J. STONE, AND M. STREITWIESER (2007): "U.S. Benchmark Input-Output Accounts, 2002," *Bureau of Economic Analysis*, 1, 1–20.

STOCKMAN, A., AND L. TESAR (1995): "Tastes and technology in a two-country model of the business cycle: explaining international comovements," *American Economic Review*, 85, 168–185.

SUBRAHMANYAM, A. (2010): "The cross-section of expected stock returns: what have we learnt from the past twenty-five years of research?," *European Financial Management*, 16 (1), 27–42.

SWAN, T. (1960): "Economic control in a dependent economy," *Economic Record*, 36, 51–66.

ZIETZ, J. (1996): "The relative price of tradables and nontradables and the U.S. trade balance," *Open Economies Review*, 7, 147–160.

7 Tables and Figures

Table 1: Model Calibration Parameters

Parameter	Symbol	Value
Preferences:		
discount rate	ρ	0.005
relative risk aversion	γ	5
elasticity of substitution	ϵ	1
weight on T good in CES utility	θ	0.5
weight on Home country in social planner problem	λ	0.5
Endowment processes for Home country:		
mean reversion rate of shock to T sector	$\theta^H_{x,T}$	0.35
volatility of shock to T sector	$\sigma^H_{x,T}$	0.04
mean reversion rate of shock to NT sector	$\theta^H_{x,NT}$	0.20
volatility of shock to NT sector	$\sigma^H_{x,NT}$	0.01
correlation of shocks to T and NT sector	δ^H_x	0.36
Endowment processes for Foreign country:		
mean reversion rate of shock to T sector	$\theta^F_{x,T}$	0.21
volatility of shock to T sector	$\sigma^F_{x,T}$	0.03
mean reversion rate of shock to NT sector	$\theta^F_{x,NT}$	0.19
volatility of shock to NT sector	$\sigma^F_{x,NT}$	0.04
correlation of shocks to T and NT sector	δ^F_x	0.78

Table 1 contains the parameters used for the calibration. The discount rate ρ is for quarterly data. Parameters for the endowment processes for the Home and Foreign country are calibrated to match actual data from 1950-2007 for the U.S. and the rest of the G7 countries respectively. Data for the U.S. is from the BEA NIPA tables and for the G7 countries (excluding U.S.) is from the IMF IFS database. The mean reversion rate and volatility of endowment shocks in the tradable sector and non-tradable sector match that in the detrended quantities of exports and quantity of GDP series respectively.

Table 2: Model Simulation Results

		median	5th	95th
(A) Excess stock returns:				
T portfolio	mean	5.9	-5.1	12.9
	std dev	22.3	17.7	24.5
NT portfolio	mean	3.9	-3.7	8.9
	std dev	15.6	13.3	17.4
$TMNT$ portfolio	mean	1.9	-1.5	4.0
	std dev	7.1	5.2	7.8
cyclicality T vs NT		1.74	1.66	1.78
	std dev	0.18	0.15	0.23
(B) Cash flow growth:				
vol T sector		6.4	6.2	7.6
vol NT sector		5.5	5.0	6.1
ratio vol T vs NT		1.19	1.05	1.41

Table 2 presents the model simulation results of stock returns and cash flow growth for the Home country. Stock returns and cash flow growth are in percent per annum. Endowment processes with a length of 50 years are generated using the calibration parameters in Table 1. The simulated data is at a quarterly frequency and then aggregated to form annual observations. For each variable, the table shows the median, 5th, and 95th percentile values over 1000 Monte Carlo simulations. $TMNT$ represents the difference in returns between the tradable (T) and non-tradable (NT) sector.

Figure 1: Model Simulation Results - Real Exchange Rate Predictability

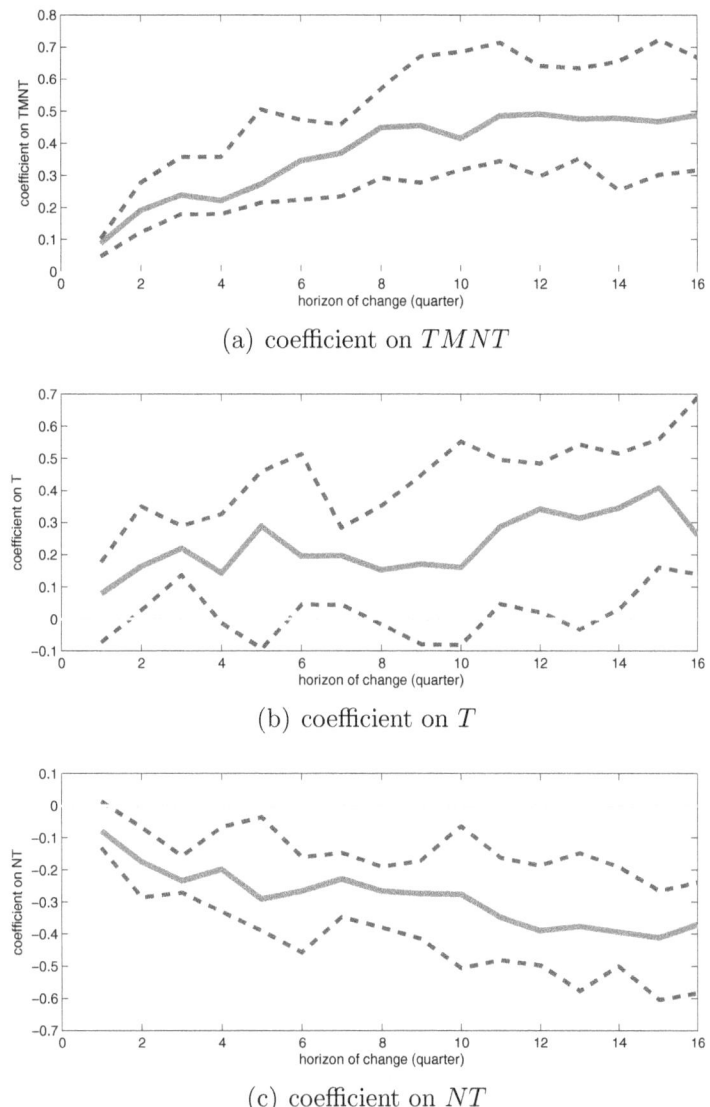

(a) coefficient on $TMNT$

(b) coefficient on T

(c) coefficient on NT

Figure 1 presents the model simulation results for exchange rate predictability using stock returns in the Home country:

$$\log(RER)_{t+h} - \log(RER)_t = \alpha_h + \beta_h R^H_{TMNT,t} + \epsilon_t$$

$$\log(RER)_{t+h} - \log(RER)_t = \alpha_h + \gamma_{T,h} R^H_{T,t} + \gamma_{NT,h} R^H_{NT,t} + \epsilon_t$$

Panel A plots the β_h coefficient from regressing the forward-looking change in the real exchange rate on the quarterly returns of the $TMNT$ portfolio, the difference in returns between the tradable (T) and non-tradable (NT) sector, for $h = 1$ to 16 quarters. Panel B and C plots the $\gamma_{T,h}$ and $\gamma_{NT,h}$ coefficients from regressing real exchange rate change on the returns of the T and NT portfolio separately. The solid line is the median coefficient, and the dotted lines are the 5th and 95th percentile coefficients over 1000 Monte Carlo simulations. T-statistics are estimated using Newey and West (1987) standard errors.

Table 3: Top and Bottom 10 Industries by Tradability Ratio

top 10:		
industry	trad ratio	description
333314	0.88	Optical instrument and lens manufacturing
114100	0.74	Fishing
333130	0.64	Mining and oil and gas field machinery manufacturing
336413	0.57	Other aircraft parts and auxiliary equipment manufacturing
33399A	0.55	Other general purpose machinery manufacturing
336412	0.54	Aircraft engine and engine parts manufacturing
333994	0.53	Industrial process furnace and oven manufacturing
334513	0.52	Industrial process variable instruments manufacturing
316100	0.51	Leather and hide tanning and finishing
334411	0.50	Electron tube manufacturing
bottom 10:		
industry	trad ratio	description
213111	0.000040	Drilling oil and gas wells
811192	0.000019	Car washes
624200	0.000017	Community food housing and other relief services
525000	0.000014	Funds, trusts, and other financial vehicles
812900	0.000012	Other personal services
812300	0.000008	Dry-cleaning and laundry services
812200	0.000004	Death care services
624400	0.000002	Child day care services
812100	0.000001	Personal care services
230101	0.000000	Nonresidential commercial and health care structures

Table 3 reports the top and bottom 10 industries by tradability ratio, computed using the 2002 BEA NIPA Input-Output Tables. The tradability ratio is defined to be the ratio of exports to total industry output.

Table 4: Tradability Ratio Summary Statistics

	industries	firms
mean	0.10	0.10
median	0.055	0.075
min	0	0
max	0.88	0.88
std dev	0.13	0.13
percentile:		
20th	0.002	0.002
40th	0.028	0.028
60th	0.083	0.089
80th	0.17	0.18
N	439	14,190

Table 4 contains summary statistics for the tradability ratio, computed using the 2002 BEA NIPA Input-Output Tables. The tradability ratio is defined to be the ratio of exports to total industry output. The statistics are computed over all 439 industries in the Input-Output Tables, as well as over the 14,190 firms in CRSP that map to these industries.

Table 5: Characteristics of Tradability-Sorted Portfolios

1950-2007	NT	2	3	4	T
num firms	2838	2838	2838	2838	2838
num industries	52	80	93	90	74
tradability ratio:					
min	0	0.002	0.03	0.09	0.18
max	0.002	0.02	0.09	0.18	0.88
median	0.001	0.02	0.08	0.12	0.26
market equity	0.13	0.10	0.20	0.14	0.09
book-to-market	0.77	0.69	0.74	0.66	0.65
leverage	0.48	0.37	0.38	0.34	0.31

Table 5 presents the average tradability ratio, proportion of market equity, book-to-market ratio, and leverage for five tradability-sorted portfolio from 1950-2007. Portfolios are listed in order of increasing tradability ratio, defined as exports over total industry output, computed using the 2002 BEA NIPA Input-Output Tables. Proportion of market equity is the ratio of total market capitalization of all firms in the portfolio over market capitalization of all firms in CRSP. Data on book-to-market ratio and leverage is from Compustat. Book-to-market ratio is book equity divided by market equity. Leverage is book liabilities divided by market value.

Table 6: Excess Returns of Tradability-Sorted Portfolios

period		NT	2	3	4	T	$TMNT$	$TMNT_2$
1950-07	mean	0.54	0.48	0.71	0.65	0.69	0.14	0.09
	t-stat	3.74	3.07	4.44	3.76	3.04	0.90	0.68
	std dev	3.8	4.2	4.2	4.6	6.0	4.2	3.3
1950-07	mean	0.42	-0.16	0.12	-0.07	-0.52	-0.94	-0.57
(rec)	t-stat	0.78	-0.31	0.21	-0.12	-0.68	-2.27	-1.52
	std dev	5.5	5.4	5.7	5.9	7.7	4.2	3.8
1950-07	mean	0.59	0.58	0.81	0.77	0.90	0.31	0.20
(exp)	t-stat	4.13	3.67	5.12	4.42	3.91	1.82	1.51
	std dev	3.5	3.9	3.9	4.3	5.7	4.2	3.3

Table 6 reports the average monthly excess returns (in percent), t-statistics, and standard deviation (in percent) for the five tradability-sorted portfolios (listed in order of increasing tradability). $TMNT$ is the returns of the tradable (quintile 5) minus non-tradable (quintile 1) portfolio. $TMNT_2$ is the returns of quintile 5 minus the average of quintiles 1 through 4. The average returns are computed over the entire sample period (1950-2007), as well as over recession and expansion periods. Recession dates are based on business cycles as determined by the NBER.

Figure 2: Annual Returns of $TMNT$

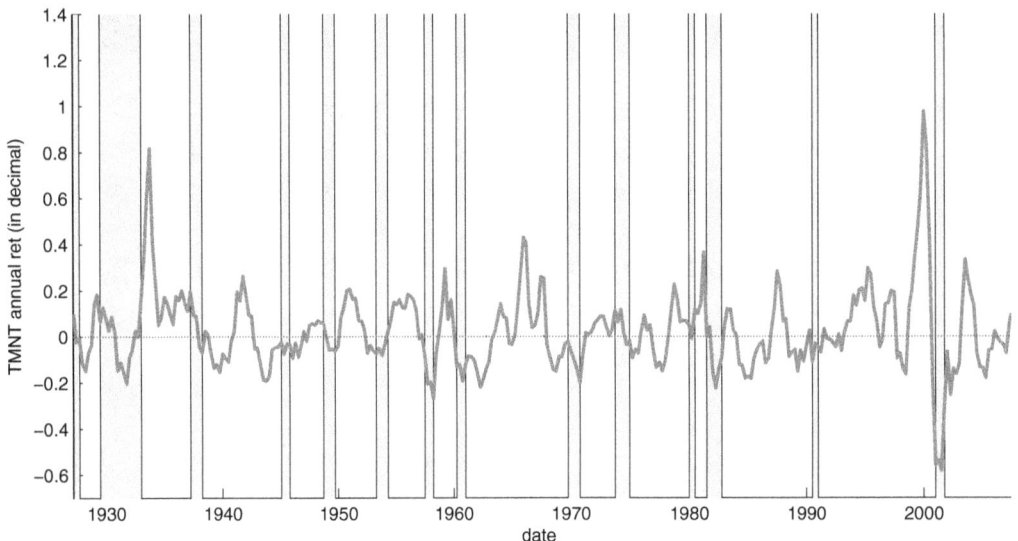

Figure 2 plots the annual returns of $TMNT$ from 1927-2007. Recession dates, based on business cycles as determined by the NBER, are shaded. $TMNT$ is the returns of the tradable (quintile 5) minus non-tradable (quintile 1) portfolio from a quintile sort of firms by tradability ratio.

Table 7: Time-Series Regressions of Tradability-Sorted Portfolios

	NT	2	3	4	T	$TMNT$
			Panel A: CAPM (1950-2007)			
α	-0.02	-0.08	0.08	0.01	-0.02	0.01
	(-0.39)	(-1.15)	(1.89)	(0.24)	(-0.21)	(0.07)
α_{rec}	0.37	0.08	0.04	-0.03	-0.20	-0.64
	(2.50)	(0.54)	(0.45)	(-0.26)	(-1.00)	(-2.24)
β^{MKT}	0.80	0.91	0.92	1.03	1.23	0.41
	(20.01)	(19.77)	(33.60)	(28.25)	(24.21)	(5.10)
β^{MKT}_{rec}	0.13	-0.074	0.004	-0.027	0.11	0.005
	(2.28)	(-1.16)	(0.10)	(-0.53)	(1.00)	(0.04)
R squared	0.84	0.84	0.91	0.90	0.82	0.22
			Panel B: FF 3 factor (1950-2007)			
α	-0.05	-0.03	0.09	0.04	0.09	0.15
	(-0.73)	(-0.47)	(2.07)	(0.86)	(0.91)	(0.98)
α_{rec}	0.34	0.04	0.04	0.00	-0.21	-0.62
	(2.04)	(0.26)	(0.46)	(-0.03)	(-1.12)	(-2.04)
β^{MKT}	0.81	0.91	0.95	1.03	1.10	0.28
	(19.54)	(18.44)	(33.49)	(26.36)	(20.12)	(3.27)
β^{MKT}_{rec}	0.12	-0.037	-0.006	-0.017	-0.066	-0.15
	(1.20)	(-0.48)	(-0.11)	(-0.29)	(-0.67)	(-0.88)
β^{SMB}	0.005	-0.078	-0.16	-0.054	0.32	0.30
	(0.08)	(-1.36)	(-3.25)	(-1.08)	(3.23)	(2.17)
β^{SMB}_{rec}	0.10	-0.004	0.081	-0.080	0.066	-0.071
	(1.13)	(-0.04)	(0.96)	(-0.70)	(0.33)	(-0.31)
β^{HML}	0.049	-0.11	-0.008	-0.066	-0.28	-0.32
	(0.63)	(-1.76)	(-0.24)	(-1.18)	(-3.20)	(-2.09)
β^{HML}_{rec}	0.067	0.12	0.006	-0.064	-0.30	-0.37
	(0.44)	(0.97)	(0.07)	(-0.64)	(-1.74)	(-1.46)
R squared	0.84	0.85	0.92	0.90	0.86	0.32

Table 7 presents results from conditional time series regressions over the sample period 1950-2007 for monthly percentage returns of five tradability-sorted portfolios (listed in order of increasing tradability). $TMNT$ is the returns of the tradable (quintile 5) minus non-tradable (quintile 1) portfolio. Panel A presents the results from the conditional CAPM regression:

$$R_{i,t} = \alpha_i + \alpha_{i,rec}d_{rec,t} + \beta_i^{MKT}R_{MKT,t} + \beta_{i,rec}^{MKT}(R_{MKT,t} * d_{rec,t}) + \epsilon_t$$

Panel B presents the results from the conditional Fama and French (1993) three-factor regression:

$$R_{i,t} = \alpha_i + \alpha_{i,rec}d_{rec,t} + \beta_i^{MKT}R_{MKT,t} + \beta_{i,rec}^{MKT}(R_{MKT,t} * d_{rec,t})$$
$$+ \beta_i^{SMB}R_{SMB,t} + \beta_{i,rec}^{SMB}(R_{SMB,t} * d_{rec,t}) + \beta_i^{HML}R_{HML,t} + \beta_{i,rec}^{HML}(R_{HML,t} * d_{rec,t}) + \epsilon_t$$

$d_{rec,t}$ is a dummy variable that is equal to 1 if the economy is in a recession during month t and equal to 0 otherwise. Recession dates are based on business cycles as determined by the NBER. T-statistics are in parentheses.

Table 8: Cyclicality of Tradability-Sorted Portfolios

1950-2007	NT	2	3	4	T	$TMNT$
GDP beta	0.90	0.90	1.12	1.22	2.11	1.21
	(1.55)	(1.71)	(1.98)	(1.94)	(2.89)	(2.32)

Table 8 reports the exposure of the five tradability-sorted portfolios (listed in order of increasing tradability) to business cycles, by computing their GDP beta over the sample period 1950-2007. $TMNT$ is the returns of the tradable (quintile 5) minus non-tradable (quintile 1) portfolio. GDP beta is the coefficient from regressing excess returns on the contemporaneous change in real U.S. GDP per capita. Data is from BEA NIPA Table 1.1.6. T-statistics are in parentheses.

Table 9: Earnings Growth of Tradability-Sorted Portfolios

Panel A: Income						
sample period		*NT*	2	3	4	*T*
1961-2007	mean	17.7	17.8	21.8	20.2	26.4
	std dev	16.1	26.5	25.3	29.1	39.9
recession pds	mean	15.2	6.7	13.9	4.0	-5.8
	std dev	12.6	30.2	21.0	29.1	42.7
expansion pds	mean	17.8	18.7	22.7	21.4	29.8
	std dev	16.3	26.1	25.6	28.4	37.6
Panel B: Earnings per share						
sample period		*NT*	2	3	4	*T*
1961-2007	mean	8.5	6.9	12.5	11.6	14.4
	std dev	12.2	25.4	25.7	27.1	63.0
recession pds	mean	5.3	0.8	5.1	-7.2	-15.2
	std dev	13.7	25.7	21.3	31.0	39.1
expansion pds	mean	8.6	7.3	13.4	13.3	17.6
	std dev	11.7	25.3	26.0	25.6	63.7
Panel C: ROA						
sample period		*NT*	2	3	4	*T*
1961-2007	mean	7.4	9.5	10.2	10.1	11.6
	std dev	14.0	31.2	22.1	23.7	33.6
recession pds	mean	0.2	-5.8	0.2	-1.9	-22.5
	std dev	6.2	31.9	24.5	28.8	35.0
expansion pds	mean	8.1	10.4	10.9	11.4	15.3
	std dev	14.3	30.7	21.2	23.2	31.0

Table 9 contains the average annual change in earnings for the five tradability-sorted portfolios (listed in order of increasing tradability). Results are presented for three different measures of earnings: income before extraordinary items, earnings per share, and return on assets (ROA). The data is available from Compustat from 1961-2007. Recession dates are based on business cycles as determined by the NBER.

Figure 3: Real Exchange Rate Predictability

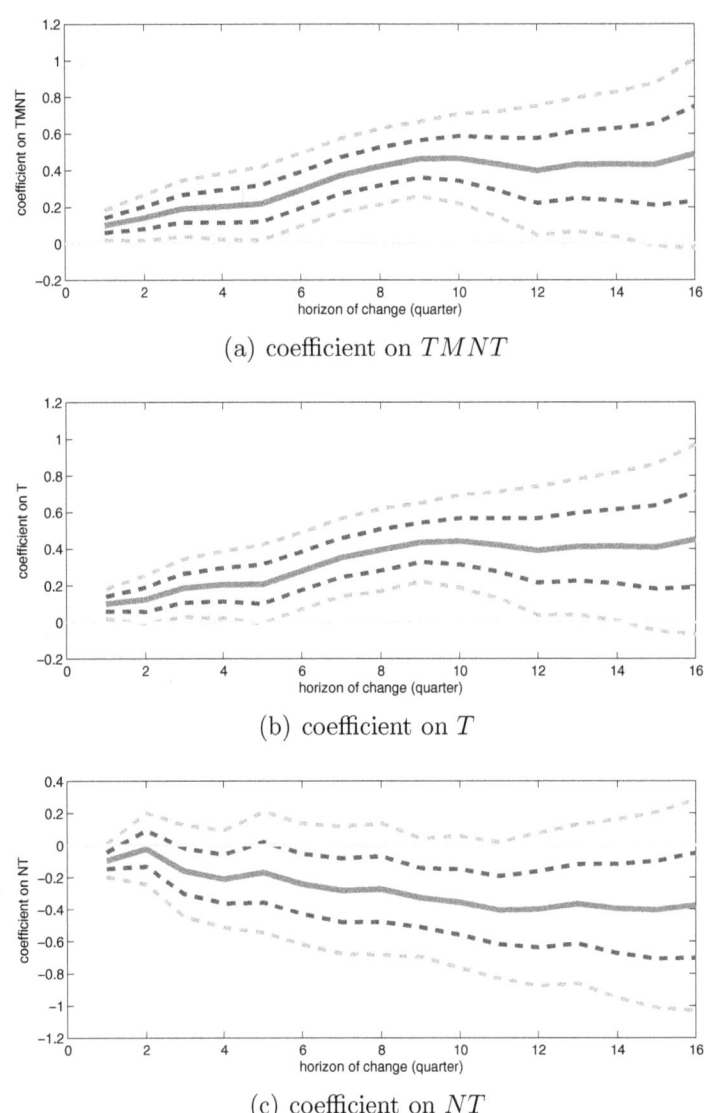

(a) coefficient on $TMNT$

(b) coefficient on T

(c) coefficient on NT

Figure 3 presents the results for real exchange rate predictability:

$$\log(RER)_{t+h} - \log(RER)_t = \alpha_h + \beta_h R_{TMNT,t} + \epsilon_t$$
$$\log(RER)_{t+h} - \log(RER)_t = \alpha_h + \gamma_{T,h} R_{T,t} + \gamma_{NT,h} R_{NT,t} + \epsilon_t$$

Panel A plots the β_h coefficient from regressing the forward-looking change in the real exchange rate (foreign currency per dollar) on quarterly returns of the $TMNT$ portfolio, for $h = 1$ to 16 quarters. The real exchange rate is constructed from data from the IMF IFS database, available at a quarterly frequency from 1968-2007. Panel B and C plots the $\gamma_{T,h}$ and $\gamma_{NT,h}$ coefficients from regressing real exchange rate change on returns of the T and NT portfolio separately. The dashed lines represent one and two standard error confidence intervals. T-statistics are estimated using Newey and West (1987) standard errors.

Robustness Table 1: Tradability Ratio Summary Statistics - 1987 BEA Table

	industries	firms
mean	0.07	0.05
median	0.03	0.02
min	0	0
max	0.60	0.60
std dev	0.08	0.07
percentile:		
20th	0.002	0.004
40th	0.02	0.02
60th	0.05	0.03
80th	0.11	0.07
N	505	18530

Robustness Table 1 contains summary statistics for the tradability ratio, computed using the 1987 BEA NIPA Input-Output Tables. The tradability ratio is defined to be the ratio of exports to total industry output. The statistics are presented over all 505 industries in the Input-Output Tables, as well as over the 18530 firms in CRSP that map to these industries.

Robustness Table 2: Excess Returns of Tradability-Sorted Portfolios - 1987 BEA Table

period		*NT*	2	3	4	*T*	*TMNT*
				portfolio			
1950-2007	mean	0.54	0.56	0.59	0.68	0.68	0.15
	t-stat	3.59	3.55	3.42	4.36	3.39	1.13
	std dev	3.9	4.2	4.6	4.1	5.3	3.4
1950-2007	mean	0.31	0.18	-0.26	-0.06	-0.32	-0.63
(rec pds)	t-stat	0.55	0.34	-0.42	-0.11	-0.46	-1.81
	std dev	5.7	5.2	6.3	5.4	7.1	3.5
1950-2007	mean	0.60	0.61	0.74	0.80	0.86	0.26
(exp pds)	t-stat	4.11	3.80	4.33	5.08	4.25	1.90
	std dev	3.6	4.0	4.3	3.9	5.0	3.4

Robustness Table 2 reports the average monthly excess returns (in percent), t-statistics, and standard deviation (in percent) for the five tradability-sorted portfolios (listed in order of increasing tradability). $TMNT$ is the returns of the tradable (quintile 5) minus non-tradable (quintile 1) portfolio. The average returns are computed over the entire sample period (1950-2007), as well as over recession and expansion periods. Recession dates are based on business cycles as determined by the NBER.

Robustness Table 3: Correlation of Tradability-Sorted Portfolios

1950-2007:	NT	2	3	4	T	$TMNT_{2002}$
NT	0.99	0.83	0.81	0.81	0.73	
2	0.83	0.94	0.84	0.82	0.82	
3	0.81	0.88	0.93	0.86	0.82	
4	0.81	0.85	0.94	0.92	0.80	
T	0.74	0.80	0.87	0.88	0.97	
$TMNT_{1987}$						0.94

Robustness Table 3 shows the correlations of the five tradability-sorted portfolios, created using the 1987 versus the 2002 BEA NIPA data. Row i column j shows the correlation of quintile i, constructed using 1987 tradability data, and quintile j, constructed using 2002 tradability data. The sample period is 1950-2007. $TMNT$ is the returns of quintile 5 (highest tradability) minus quintile 1 (lowest tradability).

Robustness Table 4: Portfolio Transition Probabilities

		2002 data				
		NT	2	3	4	T
	NT	0.71	0.16	0.08	0.04	0.02
1987 data	2	0.18	0.38	0.27	0.13	0.04
	3	0.07	0.42	0.31	0.16	0.04
	4	0.05	0.05	0.3	0.44	0.16
	T	0.01	0.03	0.07	0.2	0.69

Robustness Table 4 presents the portfolio transition probabilities for five portfolios sorted by tradability ratio using 1987 versus 2002 BEA data. Row i column j shows the probability that a firm which was sorted into quintile i using 1987 data ends up in quintile j using 2002 data.

Robustness Table 5: Composition of Tradability-Sorted Portfolios - Type of Good Produced

	NT	2	3	4	T
number of firms (durable)	14	31	191	169	239
percent of portfolio equity	0.01	0.78	2.13	3.63	2.51
number of firms (nondurable)	43	188	400	748	80
percent of portfolio equity	0.20	4.88	20.09	20.37	1.28
number of firms (services)	741	323	119	117	1
percent of portfolio equity	10.24	6.46	1.05	0.39	0.01
number of firms (investment)	85	324	501	554	1685
percent of portfolio equity	0.16	6.06	5.55	15.19	44.79
number of firms that are other	1955	1972	1627	1250	833
number of firms in quintile	2838	2838	2838	2838	2838

Robustness Table 5 contains the number of firms in each tradability-sorted portfolio that produce goods which fall into either a consumption (durables, nondurables, services) or investment industry. Portfolios are listed in order of increasing tradability ratio, defined as exports over total industry output using the 2002 BEA NIPA Input-Output Tables. Percent of portfolio equity is the proportion of total market capitalization of all firms in each category over the market capitalization of the portfolio.

Robustness Table 6: Cyclicality of Tradability-Sorted Portfolios - Within Subsets

1950-2007	NT	2	3	4	T	$TMNT$
C	0.89	0.90	0.30	1.26	2.92	2.03
	(1.11)	(1.37)	(0.43)	(1.78)	(3.62)	(3.38)
I	3.86	1.62	1.88	1.79	1.57	-2.30
	(4.05)	(1.90)	(2.79)	(1.92)	(1.94)	(-3.63)
not C	0.72	0.71	1.12	1.03	1.92	1.20
	(1.32)	(1.35)	(1.96)	(1.64)	(2.61)	(2.20)
not I	0.70	0.66	0.87	0.90	2.44	1.73
	(1.26)	(1.27)	(1.52)	(1.53)	(3.52)	(3.56)
not I and not C	0.70	0.62	1.01	0.77	2.39	1.69
	(1.27)	(1.20)	(1.76)	(1.34)	(3.46)	(3.36)

Robustness Table 6 presents the GDP betas of firms in each tradability-sorted portfolio that are in the consumption-goods (C) or investment-goods industries (I) or neither (not I and not C). Portfolios are listed in order of increasing tradability ratio, defined as exports over total industry output using the 2002 BEA NIPA Input-Output Tables. $TMNT$ is the returns of the tradable (quintile 5) minus non-tradable (quintile 1) portfolio. GDP beta is the coefficient from regressing excess returns on the contemporaneous change in real U.S. GDP per capita. Data is from BEA NIPA Table 1.1.6. Sample period is 1950-2007. T-statistics are in parentheses.

Appendix

A Tradability ratio

I use the Make and Use Tables from the 2002 BEA NIPA Input-Output Tables to compute the proportion of exports over total industry output for each industry. This proportion is the measure of tradability.

The Make Table shows how much each industry produces of each type of over 400 commodities. $make(i, c)$ denotes the dollar value of how much industry i produces of commodity c. The sum of the dollar amount produced for all commodities is the total industry output: $TIO(i) = \sum_c make(i, c)$.

The Use Table shows how each commodity is used or consumed. $use(c, i)$ denotes the dollar amount of commodity c used by industry i and $use(c, f)$ denotes the dollar amount of commodity c consumed for final uses (personal consumption, private investment, exports, imports, government consumption). In particular, I am interested in the dollar amount falling into the category of final uses for exports of goods and services: $use(c, ex)$. The sum of the dollar amounts used by each industry and for final uses is the total commodity output: $TCO(c) = \sum_i use(c, i) + \sum_f use(c, f)$.[11]

Tradability ratio for each industry i, is defined to be the ratio of exports for the industry to total industry output:

$$trad(i) = \frac{ex(i)}{TIO(i)} \tag{15}$$

where

$$ex(i) = \sum_c \frac{use(c, ex)}{TCO(c)} \cdot make(i, c)$$

Namely, the dollar amount of exports of commodity c for industry i, is equal to the proportion of how much of each commodity is exported, multiplied by $make(i, c)$. This is summed over all commodities to arrive at $ex(i)$, the dollar amount of exports for industry i.

The measure for tradability is computed for each of the 439 industries in the Input-Output Tables. To arrive at a measure for tradability at the firm level, I use the BEA's mapping of NAICS industry codes to Input-Output industries (IO code). The CRSP/ Compustat Merged Database provides a mapping of permno to NAICS. Combining these two mappings, I can assign each firm the tradability ratio for the industry that it's in.

---

[11]See Stewart, Stone, and Streitwieser (2007)

B Solution to Social Planner's Problem

The social planner chooses countries' consumption to maximize a weighted average of each country's expected utility, with weights λ and $(1 - \lambda)$ for the Home and Foreign country respectively:

$$\max_{\{c_{T,t}^i, c_{NT,t}^i\}} E_0 \left[\lambda \int_0^\infty e^{-\rho t} \frac{1}{1-\gamma} (c_t^H)^{1-\gamma} \, dt + (1 - \lambda) \int_0^\infty e^{-\rho t} \frac{1}{1-\gamma} (c_t^F)^{1-\gamma} \, dt \right] \tag{16}$$

subject to the resource constraints

$$c_{T,t}^H + c_{T,t}^F = x_{T,t}^H + x_{T,t}^F$$
$$c_{NT,t}^H = x_{NT,t}^H$$
$$c_{NT,t}^F = x_{NT,t}^F$$

where c_t^H and c_t^F are the CES consumption bundles defined in equation (2).

The first order conditions to the social planner's problem are:

$$\lambda e^{-\rho t} U'(c_{T,t}^H) = \pi_t \tag{17}$$
$$\lambda e^{-\rho t} U'(c_{NT,t}^H) = \pi_t p_{H,t} \tag{18}$$
$$(1 - \lambda) e^{-\rho t} U'(c_{T,t}^F) = \pi_t \tag{19}$$
$$(1 - \lambda) e^{-\rho t} U'(c_{NT,t}^F) = \pi_t p_{F,t} \tag{20}$$

π_t, the state price density, is the Lagrange multiplier associated with the resource constraint for the tradable good. $\pi_t p_{H,t}$ and $\pi_t p_{F,t}$ are the Lagrange multipliers for the resource constraints for the non-tradable good in each country.

The first order conditions imply

$$p_{H,t} = \frac{U'(c_{NT,t}^H)}{U'(c_{T,t}^H)} \tag{21}$$

$$p_{F,t} = \frac{U'(c_{NT,t}^F)}{U'(c_{T,t}^F)} \tag{22}$$

$$\frac{U'(c_{T,t}^H)}{U'(c_{T,t}^F)} = \frac{\lambda}{1 - \lambda} \tag{23}$$

where utility is as defined in equation (1). The equilibrium relative price of the non-tradable good is equal to the marginal rate of substitution between the tradable and non-tradable good. Because international trade of the tradable good is assumed to the costless, the ratio of the marginal utilities of the tradable good across countries depends only on λ, the welfare weight on the Home country in the social planner's problem.

Simplifying equations (21) and (22) leads to the equilibrium consumption allocations, in terms of endowments and relative prices p_H and p_F:

$$c_{T,t}^H = \left(\frac{\theta}{1-\theta}p_{H,t}\right)^\epsilon x_{NT,t}^H, \quad c_{NT,t}^H = x_{NT,t}^H \tag{24}$$

$$c_{T,t}^F = \left(\frac{\theta}{1-\theta}p_{F,t}\right)^\epsilon x_{NT,t}^F, \quad c_{NT,t}^F = x_{NT,t}^F \tag{25}$$

Substituting the consumption allocations back into the first order conditions allows us to solve for the state price density:

$$\pi_t = \frac{\lambda e^{-\rho t}}{(x_{NT,t}^H)^\gamma}\left(\frac{p_{H,t}}{1-\theta}\right)^{-\epsilon\gamma}(P_t^H)^{\epsilon\gamma-1} \tag{26}$$

where P_t^H is the price of the Home country's consumption basket in equation (3). Equivalently, the state price density can be expressed in terms of the state variables in the Foreign country:

$$\pi_t = \frac{(1-\lambda)e^{-\rho t}}{(x_{NT,t}^F)^\gamma}\left(\frac{p_{F,t}}{1-\theta}\right)^{-\epsilon\gamma}(P_t^F)^{\epsilon\gamma-1} \tag{27}$$

where P_t^F is the price of the Foreign country's consumption basket.

The first order conditions and resource constraints then reduce to a system of two equations, satisfied by relative prices $p_{H,t}$ and $p_{F,t}$:

$$\left(\frac{\theta}{1-\theta}p_{H,t}\right)^\epsilon x_{NT,t}^H + \left(\frac{\theta}{1-\theta}p_{F,t}\right)^\epsilon x_{NT,t}^F = x_{T,t}^H + x_{T,t}^F \tag{28}$$

$$\left(\frac{p_{H,t}}{p_{F,t}}\right)^\epsilon \left(\frac{\lambda}{1-\lambda}\right)^{\frac{1}{\gamma}}\left(\frac{P_t^H}{P_t^F}\right)^{\frac{\epsilon\gamma-1}{\gamma}} = \frac{x_{NT,t}^H}{x_{NT,t}^F} \tag{29}$$

www.ingramcontent.com/pod-product-compliance
Lightning Source LLC
Chambersburg PA
CBHW080615180526
45168CB00007B/2920